cute Christmas cookies

cute Christmas cookies

adorable and delicious festive treats

Hannah Miles

Photography by Steve Painter

RYLAND PETERS & SMALL
LONDON • NEW YORK

Dedication

For Charlotte, who loves baking as much as I do.

Photographer and prop stylist Steve Painter
Food stylist Lucy McKelvie
Senior designer Sonya Nathoo
Editor Kate Eddison
Production controller Mai-Ling Collyer
Art director Leslie Harrington
Editorial director Julia Charles
Publisher Cindy Richards
Indexer Hilary Bird

First published in 2017 by
Ryland Peters & Small
20–21 Jockey's Fields, London WC1R 4BW
and 341 E 116th St, New York NY 10029

www.rylandpeters.com

10 9 8 7 6 5 4 3 2 1

ISBN: 978-1-84975-888-8

Printed in China

A CIP record for this book is available
from the British Library. US Library of Congress
Cataloging-in-Publication Data has been applied for.

Notes

• Both British (Metric) and American (Imperial plus
US cups) measurements are included in these recipes
for your convenience, however it is important to work
with one set of measurements only and not alternate
between the two within a recipe.
• All spoon measurements are level unless otherwise
specified. A teaspoon is 5 ml, a tablespoon is 15 ml.
• All eggs are medium (UK) or large (US), unless
specified as large, in which case US extra-large should
be used. Uncooked or partially cooked eggs should not
be served to the very old, frail, young children, pregnant
women or those with compromised immune systems.
• Ovens should be preheated to the specified
temperatures. We recommend using an oven
thermometer. If using a fan-assisted oven, adjust
temperatures according to the manufacturer's
instructions.

Author's acknowledgments

With all my thanks to the wonderful RPS team for this
beautiful book, particularly to Steve and Lucy. As always
you worked your magic with stunning photographs and
styling – your work is too beautiful for words. Thanks
also go to Sonya for all her work on the design and
Julia for giving me the opportunity to indulge my love of
Christmas baking. Many thanks also to Kate for her
patient editing. To all my friends and family who
ate Christmas cookies even though it was
Springtime – you are the best x

Contents

Introduction

No other holiday lends itself to the fun of decorative cookies as much as Christmas does. It's the time when friends and family drop by to visit, and having festive cookies in a jar makes entertaining easy. Cookies also make perfect gifts wrapped in clear plastic film and tied with festive ribbon in a bow.

Cookies are not only good for giving and eating, but are also beautiful ornaments, which can be used to hang on your tree – bake cookie bunting to string up or festive stained glass sugar cookies to hang in a window and twinkle in the light.

For friends who deserve a special treat, why not make the hot chocolate cups? These cups and saucers are made of cookie dough with candy cane handles, filled with a rich chocolate ganache and topped with mini marshmallows.

Christmas is a time for little ones and this book contains a wide variety of cookies that children will not only love to eat but can make with you. Rudolf cookies, decorated with pretzel antlers and candy noses, will certainly be popular! They can also try their hand at carrot cookies to leave out for Santa and Rudolf on Christmas Eve. An ideal way to have fun together as a family.

Using coloured royal icing allows you to make stunning edible pictures, such as the cookie snow globes, with tiny polar bears looking up at a snow-filled sky. I also love the diamond-shaped Santas with swirling white beards and rosy cheeks.

The best thing about cookies is the short time they take to bake – only around 10 minutes. Simply turn the oven on and in no time at all you will have a kitchen filled with the delicious scents of sugar and spices, and the promise of cookies ready to eat. Make today a festive cookie day! Happy Christmas Baking. x

seasonal magic

Coconut snowballs

FOR THE COOKIES

30 g/2½ tablespoons caster/
   granulated sugar
60 g/½ stick butter, softened
90 g/⅔ cup plain/all-
   purpose flour, sifted, plus
   extra for dusting
1 tablespoon cream cheese
60 g/generous ¾ cup soft
   shredded coconut

FOR THE MERINGUE

2 UK large/US extra large
   egg whites
115 g/generous ½ cup
   caster/granulated sugar
1 teaspoon pure vanilla
   extract or ½ teaspoon
   vanilla bean powder
9 mini coconut chocolates,
   such as Bounty bars or
   Mounds, cut in half
60 g/generous ¾ cup soft
   shredded coconut
5-cm/2-inch round cutter
2 large baking sheets,
   greased and lined
ice cream scoop

Makes 18

Powdery snow is one of the highlights of winter – perfect for sledging and snowball fights. These are my snowball cookies – with a crisp coconut cookie base, topped with a gooey coconut meringue and a hidden coconut-chocolate surprise inside. Perfect for serving with hot chocolate after a chilly snowball fight. If you do not have mini Bounties or Mounds, use two regular bars instead and cut each into nine pieces.

Begin by making the coconut cookies. In a mixing bowl, whisk together the caster/granulated sugar and butter until soft and creamy. Add the flour and cream cheese and mix to a soft dough. Fold in the coconut. Wrap the dough in clingfilm/plastic wrap and chill in the refrigerator for 30 minutes.

Preheat the oven to 180°C (350°F) Gas 4.

On a flour-dusted surface, roll out the dough thinly. Cut out 18 rounds of cookie dough using the cutter and place on the prepared baking sheets, leaving space between them. Bake for about 8–10 minutes until golden brown. Leave to cool on the baking sheets.

Turn the oven temperature down to the lowest setting, around 100°C (200°F) Gas ¼. It is important that the temperature has dropped completely from cooking the cookies before you cook the meringue, otherwise the meringue will turn a caramel colour rather than staying white like a snowball.

In a clean, dry bowl, whisk the egg whites to stiff peaks. Add the sugar into the meringue a spoonful at a time, whisking all the time. Whisk until all the sugar is incorporated and you have a smooth, glossy meringue. Whisk in the vanilla.

Place a piece of mini Bounty or Mounds into the centre of each cookie. Using the ice cream scoop, place scoops of meringue on top of each cookie, making sure the Bounty or Mounds piece is covered. Sprinkle the meringue with the soft shredded coconut. Bake in the oven for about 1–1½ hours until the meringues are crisp on the outside but are still white in colour and have a gooey centre.

These cookies will keep for up to 3 days in an airtight container.

FOR THE COOKIES

115 g/1 stick butter, softened

200 g/1 cup caster/
   granulated sugar

2¹/₂ tablespoons espresso

1 egg

1 pinch salt

1 teaspoon pure vanilla
   extract or ¹/₂ teaspoon
   vanilla bean powder

280 g/generous 2 cups
   self-raising/self-rising
   flour, plus extra for dusting

FOR THE ICING

400 g/3 cups royal icing/
   confectioners' sugar, sifted

60–80 ml/¹/₄–¹/₃ cup
   espresso

18 edible transfers

2 baking sheets, greased
   and lined

piping/pastry bag fitted with
   a small round nozzle/tip
   or a small leaf nozzle/tip
   for a ruffled effect

Makes 18

Coffee cookies with vintage edible transfers

In this age of modern technology, there are some wonderful products to enhance your baking, such as edible printed icing or rice paper sheets that allow you to create stunning effects on cakes and cookies.

In a mixing bowl, whisk together the butter and sugar until light and creamy. Add the cold espresso coffee and whisk in with the egg. Add the salt, vanilla and flour, and whisk until you have a soft dough. Wrap the dough in clingfilm/plastic wrap and chill in the refrigerator for 30 minutes.

Preheat the oven to 180°C (350°F) Gas 4.

On a flour-dusted surface, roll out the dough to about 5 mm/¼ inch thickness. I work with half of the dough at a time, cutting out nine rectangles (about 12 x 8 cm/ 5 x 3 inches) from each portion of dough, and rerolling as necessary. Use a sharp knife to cut out the rectangles and transfer them to the prepared baking sheets using a spatula. The actual size you need for your cookies will depend on the size of transfers you are using. The cookies will expand a little during baking, so cut to the size of your transfers, then when baked, there should be a small border for the icing.

Bake for 10–15 minutes until lightly golden brown, taking care as the coffee cookies can turn dark quickly. Transfer to a cooling rack and leave to cool completely.

For the icing, whisk the icing/confectioners' sugar and coffee together in a bowl (adding the coffee gradually as you may not need it all) until you have a stiff icing. Working in batches, use a round-bladed knife to spread a thin layer of icing over the top of each cookie and press on a transfer. Spoon the remaining icing into the piping/pastry bag and pipe fine lines or ruffles of icing around the edge of the pictures. Leave to set.

These cookies will store for up to 5 days in an airtight container.

Clementine linzer sandwiches

140 g/scant ¾ cup caster/
   granulated sugar
125 g/9 tablespoons butter,
   softened
1 egg
250 g/generous 1¾ cups
   plain/all-purpose flour,
   sifted, plus extra for
   dusting
grated zest of 2 clementines
1 teaspoon ground
   cinnamon
icing/confectioners' sugar,
   for dusting
8 tablespoons clementine
   curd

2 baking sheets, greased
   and lined
linzer cookie cutter or
   5-cm/2-inch round cutter
   and small heart or flower
   cutters for the centre

Makes 24

Linzer cookies are classic Austrian cookies sandwiched with delicious fillings. The cookies in this recipe are flavoured with clementine zest and a pinch of cinnamon for a truly festive feel. I have filled them with clementine curd, but you can use orange or lemon curd if you cannot find a clementine curd. Alternatively, omit the clementine zest and sandwich pairs of cookies around thick salted caramel sauce or dulce de leche for equally delicious results.

Preheat the oven to 180°C (350°F) Gas 4.

In a large mixing bowl, whisk together the caster/granulated sugar and softened butter until light and creamy. Add the egg and whisk in. Add the flour, zest and cinnamon and whisk in to form a stiff dough. Wrap in clingfilm/plastic wrap and chill in the refrigerator for 30 minutes.

On a flour-dusted surface, roll out the dough to about 5 mm/¼ inch thickness. Cut out 48 circles using the cutter. Leave 24 cookies whole and cut out centre holes from the other 24 cookies using the linzer cutter or a small heart or flower cutter.

Transfer to the baking sheets and bake for 10–12 minutes until crisp and light golden brown. Leave to cool completely on a cooling rack.

When cool, dust the cookies that have holes in them with a light coating of icing/confectioners' sugar. It is important to dust with icing/confectioners' sugar before sandwiching the cookies, otherwise the sugar will cover the pretty filling.

Place a teaspoon of curd in the middle of each of the whole cookies and spread out gently. Top with a sugar-dusted cookie (with a hole in).

These cookies will store for up to 3 days in an airtight container, but for the best results, assemble the cookies with the filling just before serving.

Hot chocolate cups with candy cane handles

One of the nicest things on a cold frosty day is coming home after a walk for a cup of hot chocolate with melting marshmallows on top. These pretty little cups are inspired by that delightful treat.

FOR THE COOKIES

125 g/9 tablespoons butter, softened
100 g/³/₄ cup icing/confectioners' sugar, sifted
1 egg yolk
180 g/1¹/₃ cups plain/all-purpose flour, sifted, plus extra for dusting
pinch of salt
a little milk, if needed

FOR THE FILLING

90 g/3¹/₄ oz. dark/bittersweet chocolate
30 g/¹/₄ stick butter
90 ml/¹/₃ cup double/heavy cream

FOR THE DECORATION

200 g/1¹/₂ cups royal icing/confectioners' sugar, sifted
6 candy canes
12 mini marshmallows
10-cm/4-inch round cutter
9-cm/3¹/₂-inch flower cutter
6-hole muffin pan, greased
baking beans
piping/pastry bag fitted with a small round nozzle/tip

Makes 6

Whisk together the butter and icing/confectioners' sugar until light and creamy. Whisk in the egg yolk and mix well. Add the flour and salt, and bring together to a soft dough. If the mixture is too crumbly add a little milk to bind the dough. Wrap in clingfilm/plastic wrap and chill in the refrigerator for 30 minutes.

Preheat the oven to 180°C (350°F) Gas 4.

On a flour-dusted surface roll out the dough thinly. Cut out six circles using the round cutter and six using the flower cutter. Place the flower cookies on a baking sheet and bake for 8–10 minutes until lightly golden brown. Press the six smaller round cookies into six of the holes of the greased muffin pan, and press out thinly so that the cups are filled to the top. Line each cookie with a small square of greaseproof paper and fill with baking beans. Bake for 10–12 minutes until crisp and golden, and then leave to cool completely in the pan. Once cool, remove the baking beans and paper and, using a teaspoon or sharp knife, carefully lift the cookie cups from the pan.

In a small mixing bowl, mix the royal icing/confectioners' sugar with 2–3 tablespoons water until you have a thick icing that holds a peak. Spoon into the piping/pastry bag and pipe a blob of icing into the centre of each flower cookie. Press a cookie cup on top. Pipe decorative patterns around the rim of the cup. Carefully cut the curved ends off the candy canes for the handles. Attach to the cup with a little icing and leave to set.

For the ganache, melt the chocolate with the butter and cream in a heatproof bowl set over a pan of barely simmering water. Whisk together until you have a smooth, thick ganache. Pour into the cups. Decorate with mini marshmallows and leave to set.

These cookies are best eaten on the day they are made, due to the ganache. However you can make the cookies 3 days in advance, then fill them the day you serve them.

Sugar sprinkle stars

Sometimes simplicity is best. At Christmas things are often highly decorated and iced and it can be a really indulgent time. These star cookies with citrus bursts taste delicious and are decorated very simply with coloured sugar. The sugar gives a really nice crunchy texture to the cookie and you can use any colours you wish. If you want to use these cookies as tree decorations, simply cut a small hole in them using a large round icing nozzle/tip prior to baking, then thread ribbon through when they are cool. Use a range of different sized cutters, if you wish, to create stacks of twinkling stars that resemble trees!

125 g/9 tablespoons
  butter, softened
80 g/6¹/₂ tablespoons caster/
  granulated sugar
1 egg, beaten
200 g/1¹/₂ cups plain/
  all-purpose flour, plus
  extra for dusting
grated zest of 1 lemon
1 teaspoon pure vanilla
  extract or ¹/₂ teaspoon
  vanilla bean powder
coloured crystal sugar
2 large baking sheets, lined
  with silicon mats or baking
  parchment
various star cutters

Makes about 24

In a mixing bowl whisk together the butter and sugar until light and creamy. Whisk in the egg. Sift in the flour and mix in well until you have a soft dough, adding the lemon zest and vanilla. Wrap the dough in clingfilm/plastic wrap and chill in the refrigerator for about 30 minutes.

Preheat the oven to 180°C (350°F) Gas 4.

On a flour-dusted surface, roll out the dough to about 5 mm/¼ inch thickness. Cut out star shapes and place on the prepared baking sheets a small distance apart so that they are not touching. Place small stars on one baking sheet and large stars on the other, as the smaller ones will cook more quickly.

Sprinkle each star with a little coloured sugar and bake for 10–15 minutes until the cookies start to turn light golden brown, removing the smaller cookies before the larger cookies to ensure even cooking. Leave to cool on cooling racks before serving.

These cookies will store for up to 5 days in an airtight container.

Frosted pine cones

125 g/9 tablespoons
  butter, softened
80 g/6½ tablespoons caster/
  granulated sugar
1 egg
180 g/generous ¾ cup
  plain/all-purpose flour,
  sifted
50 g/½ cup unsweetened
  cocoa powder
150 g/scant 1¼ cups
  marcona or whole
  blanched almonds
100 g/1¼ cups flaked/
  slivered almonds
icing/confectioners' sugar,
  for dusting
1 large baking sheet,
  lined with a silicon mat
  or baking parchment

Makes 15

Walking through a forest on a crisp winter's morning is a joyful experience, feeling the crunch of twigs and leaves below your feet, smelling fresh moss and hearing rustling noises of hidden animals. I love to collect pine cones which have fallen from the trees and place them in large bowls to decorate the house for Christmas. These realistic pine cone cookies make a pretty centrepiece for a party table or can be used to decorate a festive yule log cake. I am not going to lie, adding the almond flakes to each cookie takes time to get the pretty effect, so this is a job to do accompanied by a few friends and a large glass of mulled wine to keep you all going!

In a mixing bowl, whisk together the butter and sugar until light and creamy. Whisk in the egg, then sift in the flour and cocoa to make a firm dough. Wrap in clingfilm/plastic wrap and chill in the refrigerator for an hour.

Unwrap the dough and break off small pieces and mould to make 15 cone shapes, each about 5 cm/2 inches high. Place on the prepared baking sheet.

Next you need to make the cone effect using the almonds. First make two rows of whole almonds around the base of each cone, pressing them into the dough so that they are held firm. Next, make rows of flaked/slivered almonds in rings around each cone, continuing until you reach the top. Repeat with all the remaining cones.

Preheat the oven to 150°C (300°F) Gas 2.

Bake for 15–20 minutes. If any of the almonds come out whilst baking, carefully press them in again while the cookie is still warm. Allow to cool on the baking sheet.

Once cool, dust the cookies with a generous dusting of icing/confectioners' sugar to serve. These cookies will store for up to 3 days in an airtight container.

Red velvet snowcaps

100 g/3¹/₂ oz. dark/
 bittersweet chocolate,
 melted and cooled
250 g/generous 1³/₄ cups
 plain/all-purpose flour,
 sifted
2 teaspoons baking powder
pinch of salt
1 teaspoon pure vanilla
 extract or ¹/₂ teaspoon
 vanilla bean powder
100 g/¹/₂ cup caster/
 granulated sugar
1 egg, beaten
115 g/1 stick butter,
 softened
2 teaspoons red food
 colouring gel
icing/confectioners' sugar,
 for dusting, sifted
2 baking sheets, greased
 and lined

Makes 30

Snowcaps are cookies that have a decorative surface made by dusting them liberally with icing/confectioners' sugar to create a crackled effect on top when they bake. They are said to be inspired by snow-topped mountains. Traditionally chocolate, these are my red velvet version.

Add all the ingredients (excluding the icing/confectioners' sugar) into a bowl and whisk together to a soft dough. Use enough red food colouring gel to make a vibrant red colour. (I use food colour gels rather than liquids as you can achieve a richer colour with them.) You should be able to mould the dough into balls in your hands without it being too sticky, but if it is too soft, either chill it in the refrigerator or dust with a little extra flour as you work.

Preheat the oven to 180°C (350°F) Gas 4.

Roll the dough into 30 balls about the size of large walnuts. Roll each ball in icing/confectioners' sugar. Place a small distance apart on the baking sheets and sift again with a generous layer of icing/confectioners' sugar. It is important for there to be plenty of icing/confectioners' sugar as this is what makes the pretty decoration on top of the cookies when they crack open.

Bake for 10–15 minutes until the tops have cracked. Remove from the oven and leave to cool on a cooling rack.

These cookies will store for up to 5 days in an airtight container.

Iced mitten cookies

Make these adorable mitten cookies and tie them in pairs for a fun gift. If you do not have a mitten cutter, simply cut out a mitten-shape template from card and cut the dough around it using a sharp knife.

60 g/¹/₃ cup soft dark brown sugar

115 g/1 stick butter, softened

1 heaped tablespoon cream cheese

170 g/1¹/₄ cups plain/ all-purpose flour, sifted, plus extra for dusting

FOR THE DECORATION

350 g/1¹/₂ cups royal icing/ confectioners' sugar, sifted

4–5 tablespoons soft shredded coconut

mitten-shaped cookie cutter (optional)

1 large baking sheet, greased and lined

1 piping/pastry bag with a small round nozzles/tip

decorative string/twine

Makes 10

Whisk together the brown sugar and butter until soft and creamy. Add the cream cheese and flour and mix to a soft dough. Wrap the dough in clingfilm/plastic wrap and chill in the refrigerator for 1 hour.

Preheat the oven to 180°C (350°F) Gas 4.

On a flour-dusted surface, roll out the dough thinly to about 5 mm/¼ inch thickness and cut out 10 mitten cookie shapes. Carefully transfer the cookies to the prepared baking sheet. Bake for 10–12 minutes in the preheated oven until the cookies turn light golden brown. As soon as you remove the cookies from the oven, use the round icing nozzle/ tip to stamp out a hole in each cookie to thread the string/twine through. Leave the cookies on the baking sheet for a few minutes, then transfer to a cooling rack.

To decorate, place one-third of the icing/confectioners' sugar in a bowl and mix with a few teaspoons of cold water to make a stiff, thick icing. Spoon the icing into a piping/ pastry bag and pipe a line as close to the edge of the cookie as possible. Leave the outline to dry for a few minutes before flooding the cookies. To do this mix the remaining icing/confectioners' sugar with a few tablespoons of water to make a runny icing. Spread enough icing onto the cookie so that it looks generously covered, but not so much that it overflows and keep it away from the edges. Use a round-bladed knife to guide the icing so that it floods any gaps. While the icing is still wet, sprinkle the coconut across the bottom of each mitten to resemble a fluffy cuff. Leave to set completely.

Once the icing is set, use the remaining stiff icing in the piping bag to pipe decorative knitted patterns onto each of the mittens as shown. Leave the icing to set before threading onto string/twine and knotting them in pairs.

The cookies will store for up to 5 days in an airtight container. It is best to store the cookies flat, in single layers, between sheets of baking parchment.

festive friends

Snowmen faces

'Do you want to build a snowman?' So the popular movie song goes...
Well, if you do, then why not make these friendly snowy faces! The
cookies are made with marzipan and cocoa and taste scrumptious.

200 g/7 oz. natural marzipan
90 g/³⁄₄ stick butter, softened
100 g/1 cup ground
*   almonds*
100 g/³⁄₄ cup self-raising/
*   self-rising flour, plus extra*
*   for dusting*
40 g/scant ¹⁄₂ cup
*   unsweetened cocoa*
*   powder*
350 g/2¹⁄₂ cups fondant
*   icing/confectioners' sugar,*
*   sifted*
orange and black food
*   colouring gels*

7-cm/2³⁄₄-inch round cutter
2 baking sheets, lined with
*   baking parchment or*
*   silicon mats*
piping/pastry bag fitted with
*   a small round nozzle/tip*
cocktails sticks/toothpicks

Makes 20

Preheat the oven to 180°C (350°F) Gas 4.

Break the marzipan into small pieces and cream together with the butter using an
electric hand-held whisk (or in a stand mixer if preferred) until the mixture becomes
paste-like. Add the ground almonds, flour and cocoa, and beat to a smooth, soft
dough. The mixture should be soft but not sticky, so add a little more flour if needed.

On a flour-dusted surface, roll out the dough to about 5 mm/¼ inch thickness and cut
out 20 circles, rerolling the dough as necessary. Use plenty of flour to dust so that the
dough does not stick. Place the cookies on the baking sheets a small distance apart
as they will spread a little during cooking. Bake for 10–15 minutes, then remove from
the oven. Allow to cool on the baking sheets for a few minutes, then transfer to
a cooling rack to cool completely.

To ice the cookies mix 300 g/2 cups of the icing/confectioners' sugar with about
2 tablespoons of water until you have a very thick icing. Spoon about one-third of
the icing into the piping/pastry bag and pipe a circle around the edge of each cookie.
Leave to set for 10 minutes. Return any icing to the bowl and add a little more water so
that the icing is runny enough to just flow when you spoon it. Place a spoonful of icing
into each of the circles making sure that the circle is completed flooded. Leave to set.

Mix the remaining 50 g/½ cup icing/confectioners' sugar with a little water, add
a few drops of orange food colouring gel and mix well to create a bright orange. Using
a cocktail stick/toothpick or piping bag, place a line of orange icing in the centre of
each cookie to make a carrot nose. When you have completed all the noses, add a few
drops of black food colouring to the orange icing, enough to make it completely black.
Using a second cocktail stick/toothpick, place dots of black icing onto the cookies for
the eyes and mouth. Leave to set.

These cookies will store for up to 5 days in an airtight container.

Santa cookies

These festive Santas are decorated using royal icing. Simple diamond-shaped cookies give the perfect shape for Santa's hat and beard.

Whisk together the butter and sugar until light and creamy. Sift in the flour and whisk in with the clementine zest until you have a soft dough, adding a little milk if needed. Wrap in clingfilm/plastic wrap and chill in the refrigerator for 30 minutes. Preheat the oven to 180°C (350°F) Gas 4.

On a flour-dusted surface, roll out the dough to about 5 mm/¼ inch thickness and cut out 10 diamonds with 8 cm/3¼ inch sides using a sharp knife. Transfer them to the baking sheets using a spatula. Reroll the dough as necessary. Bake for 10–15 minutes until the cookies are lightly golden brown. Transfer to a cooling rack to cool completely.

Whisk the icing/confectioners' sugar with 3–4 tablespoons of water until you have a stiff icing that holds a peak. Set aside two-thirds of this icing. Colour the remaining icing red. Spoon 2 large spoonfuls of red icing into a piping/pastry bag. Spoon 5 large spoonfuls of white icing into another. Take the red icing bag and pipe a fine red line along the top edge of each cookie, following the triangle shape. Take the white icing bag and pipe the outline of the band of Santa's hat along the base of each red triangle, then pipe a half-egg shape below that to create the outline for Santa's face.

Scrape all of the red icing back into its bowl and about half of the white icing back into its bowl (reserving enough in the piping bag to pipe the beards on later). Add a little water to both the icings so that they are now thin enough to flow. Spoon a little white icing into a small bowl and add enough red to create a pale pink. Flood a little pink icing in the piped half-egg face shape on each cookie. Do the same with the red icing in the hat outline, and then the white icing in the band of the hat outline. Dip a cocktail stick/toothpick into the red icing and swirl to add rosy cheeks. Add some black food colouring to the remaining pink icing and use a cocktail stick/toothpick to add dots for eyes. Finally pipe a white curly beard in the bottom of each cookie. Pipe a small blob of icing to the top of each hat and affix a sprinkle. Allow to set for 15 minutes.

These will store for up to 5 days in an airtight container.

FOR THE COOKIES

115 g/1 stick butter,
   softened
60 g/5 tablespoons caster/
   granulated sugar
170 g/1¼ cups plain/
   all-purpose flour, sifted,
   plus extra for dusting
grated zest of 2 clementines
a little milk, if needed

FOR THE DECORATION

400 g/scant 3 cups royal
   icing/confectioners' sugar,
   sifted
red and black food
   colouring gels
large white snowflake
   sprinkles, or similar
2 baking sheets, greased
   and lined
disposable piping/pastry
   bags
cocktail sticks/toothpicks

Makes 10

Reindeer cookies

320 g/scant 2¹/₂ cups
self-raising/self-rising flour

30 g/¹/₃ cup unsweetened
cocoa powder

1 teaspoon bicarbonate of
soda/baking soda

200 g/1 cup caster/
granulated sugar

175 g/1¹/₂ sticks butter

3 heaped tablespoons
golden syrup/light corn
syrup

36 pretzels

17 sugar-coated chocolate
peanuts plus 1 red one
for Rudolf

30 g/1 oz. white chocolate,
broken into pieces

30 g/1 oz. dark/bittersweet
chocolate, broken into
pieces

3 baking sheets, greased
and lined

2 piping/pastry bags fitted
with small round nozzles/
tips

Makes 18

These festive little reindeer would make any Christmas party a jolly event – they have pretzel antlers and chocolate peanut noses – perfect for guiding Santa on his way! I have used plain pretzels but you can use yogurt- or chocolate-coated pretzels if you wish to make a variety of different reindeer. You can give all the reindeer red noses, if you wish, or just give one a red nose to represent the hero of the day Rudolf!

Preheat the oven to 180°C (350°F) Gas 4.

Sift the flour, cocoa powder and bicarbonate of soda into a mixing bowl. Stir in the sugar. In a saucepan, heat the butter and syrup until the butter has melted. Stir the syrup mixture into the flour and whisk in until the dough comes together.

Divide the dough into 18 pieces and place them in small mounds a distance apart on the baking sheets, as the cookies will spread during cooking. Press each cookie down to flatten them.

Bake in the oven for 5 minutes then remove from the oven and press two pretzels into each cookie for the antlers. Using a clean cloth press each cookie down. Return to the oven and bake for a further 5–7 minutes. Remove from the oven and immediately press one sugar-coated chocolate peanut into each cookie for the nose. Leave the cookies to cool on the baking sheets for 5 minutes, as they will be soft when you remove them from the oven, then using a spatula, transfer them to a cooling rack to cool completely.

Place the white and dark/bittersweet chocolate into two separate heatproof bowls and rest each bowl over a pan of simmering water. Heat until the chocolate has melted. Leave to cool slightly, then spoon into the piping/pastry bags.

Pipe two small circles of white chocolate onto each cookie as eyes and then pipe a smaller dot of dark chocolate onto the white chocolate. Leave to cool completely until the chocolate has set.

The cookies will store for up to 5 days in an airtight container.

Polar bear snow globes

FOR THE COOKIES

115 g/1 stick butter,
    softened
60 g/5 tablespoons caster/
    granulated sugar
170 g/1¼ cups plain/
    all-purpose flour, plus
    extra for dusting
1 teaspoon pure vanilla
    extract
pinch of salt
a little milk, if needed

FOR THE DECORATION

500 g/generous 3½ cups
    royal icing/confectioners'
    sugar, sifted
blue and black food
    colouring gel
3 piping/pastry bags, one
    fitted with a round nozzle/
    tip and one with a star
    nozzle/tip
9-cm/3½-inch round cutter
8-cm/3¼-inch round cutter
2 baking sheets, lined with
    silicon mats or baking
    parchment
cocktail sticks/toothpicks

Makes 6

I have loved snow globes ever since I was a child. There is something magical about watching a glittering snowfall settle on a wintery scene.

On a sheet of baking parchment draw eight polar bears, 4 cm/1¾ inches in length. This gives you two spares. Whisk 100 g/¾ cup of the icing/confectioners' sugar with a few teaspoons of water until you have a thick, stiff icing. Using a piping/pastry bag with a round nozzle/tip, pipe the outline of the bears. Leave to dry for a few minutes. Add a little more water to make the icing slightly runnier and spoon into the outlines. Use a cocktail stick/toothpick to help the icing fill the shape. Add black food colouring to the icing and, using a cocktail stick/toothpick, add an eye and nose. Leave to set.

Cream together the butter and sugar, then sift in the flour and mix to a soft dough. Add the vanilla and salt. Add a little milk, if needed. Wrap the dough in clingfilm/plastic wrap and chill in the refrigerator for 30 minutes. Preheat the oven to 180°C (350°F) Gas 4.

On a flour-dusted surface, roll out the dough to about 5 mm/¼ inch thickness. Cut out six rounds with the large cutter and transfer to a baking sheet. Use the smaller round cutter to cut out and remove the centre, leaving a ring of dough. Reroll the dough and press the large round cutter about three-quarters of the way into the dough six times. Don't press it all the way around as you need to cut out the base of the snow globe. Using a sharp knife, cut out a curved rectangle along the uncut section of the circle. Transfer to a baking sheet. Bake for 10–15 minutes until lightly golden brown. The rings will cook more quickly so check them often. Carefully transfer to a cooling rack to cool.

Place the remaining icing/confectioners' sugar in a mixing bowl and add about 65 ml/ ¼ cup of water until you have a smooth, thick icing. Colour half of the icing blue.

Pipe a ring of the blue icing around the edge of the globe cookies and leave for a few minutes. Add a little more water to the blue icing so that it just starts to run and spoon into the six blue rings to fill them, using a cocktail stick/toothpick to help move the icing. Place a polar bear on each globe and use a cocktail stick/ toothpick to add dots of the white icing to resemble snow. Place the cookie rings on top. Pipe white icing on the base of the snow globe using the star nozzle/tip. Keep for 5 days in an airtight container.

Gingerbread Viennese whirl sandwich cookies

FOR THE COOKIES

175 g/1½ sticks butter,
    softened
55 g/generous ⅓ cup icing/
    confectioners' sugar,
    sifted, plus extra for
    dusting
175 g/1⅓ cups plain/
    all-purpose flour, sifted
60 ml/¼ cup gingerbread
    syrup
1 teaspoon gingerbread
    spice mix or ground
    cinnamon

FOR THE FILLING

300 g/2 cups icing/
    confectioners' sugar,
    sifted
30 g/¼ stick butter, softened
30 g/1 oz. cream cheese
1 tablespoon gingerbread
    syrup
2 baking sheets, lined with
    baking parchment
2 piping/pastry bags fitted
    with large star nozzles/tips

Makes 14

I love Viennese whirls – light and crumbly cookies that just melt in the mouth. These are flavoured with gingerbread spices for a festive flavour. If you do not have gingerbread syrup, use ginger syrup instead or any other flavoured syrup of your choosing, such as cinnamon or vanilla.

Preheat the oven to 180°C (350°F) Gas 4.

In a mixing bowl, cream together the butter and icing/confectioners' sugar. The butter must be very soft, otherwise the dough will be difficult to pipe. Add the flour, syrup and spice, and whisk until you have a smooth, soft dough.

Spoon the dough into one of the piping/pastry bags and pipe 28 rosettes or swirls of the dough onto the baking sheets. The cookies will spread, so make sure that you leave gaps between them.

Bake for 10–12 minutes until golden brown. Watch carefully towards the end of cooking as they can turn dark brown quickly. Leave the cookies to cool on a cooling rack. I do this by lifting the baking parchment sheet carefully onto a cooling rack.

For the filling, whisk together the icing/confectioners' sugar, butter, cream cheese and syrup until light and creamy. Spoon into the second piping/pastry bag and chill in the refrigerator until the icing becomes firm.

Bring the icing to room temperature, then pipe a swirl of icing onto the flat side of half of the cookies, then sandwich them together with the uniced cookies. Place in cake cases to serve and dust with a little icing/confectioners' sugar.

These cookies will keep for 3 days in an airtight container.

FOR THE COOKIES

60 g/5 tablespoons caster/
   granulated sugar
115 g/1 stick butter, softened
170 g/1¼ cups plain/
   all-purpose flour, sifted,
   plus extra for dusting
1 tablespoon milk

FOR THE DECORATION

200 g/7 oz. white chocolate
orange and green food
   colouring gel
carrot cookie cutter
large baking sheet, greased
   and lined
2 piping/pastry bags fitted
   with small round nozzles/
   tips

Makes 16

Carrots for Rudolf

My niece and nephew Hunter and Bowen who live in America enjoy the tradition of leaving cookies and milk out for Santa's visit on Christmas Eve. Here in the UK I leave a sherry and a mince pie for Santa to help him on his way! Universal, though, is leaving carrots for his reindeer.

Whisk together the caster/granulated sugar and butter until soft and creamy. Add the flour and milk and mix to a soft dough. Wrap the dough in clingfilm/plastic wrap and chill in the refrigerator for 30 minutes.

Preheat the oven to 180°C (350°F) Gas 4.

On a flour-dusted surface, roll out the dough to about 5 mm/¼ inch thickness and cut out 16 carrot shapes using a cookie cutter. If you do not have a carrot cutter, cut a template out of cardboard and then cut round the template on the dough using a sharp knife. Place the cookies on a baking sheet and bake for 10–12 minutes, taking care towards the end of cooking as you do not want the cookies to turn brown. Leave on the baking sheet to cool for a few minutes, then transfer to a cooling rack.

Break the white chocolate into pieces and put it in a heatproof bowl. Rest the bowl over a pan of simmering water until the chocolate is melted, then remove it from the heat and leave it to cool for a few minutes. Colour two-thirds of the white chocolate orange and one-third green.

Place a small amount of each coloured chocolate into a piping/pastry bag. Pipe the outline of the carrot in orange and the outline of the leaves in green. Leave for a few minutes to set before filling the orange carrots with the remaining orange chocolate and filling the green tops with the remaining green chocolate.

Leave in a cool place for the chocolate to set, then store in an airtight container for up to 3 days.

Snowflake cookies

125 g/9 tablespoons
butter, softened
100 g/¹/₂ cup caster/
granulated sugar
60 g/scant ¹/₄ cup cream
cheese
1 egg
170 g/1¹/₄ cups plain/
all-purpose flour, sifted,
plus extra for dusting
icing/confectioners' sugar,
for dusting
piping/pastry bag fitted with
a small round nozzle/tip
2 baking sheets, lined with
silicon mats or baking
parchment

Makes 15

The true beauty of snowflakes is that each one of the tiny icy shapes is unique. When you look at them closely they are spectacularly pretty and intricate. The light cream-cheese enriched cookie dough in this recipe can be piped into pretty shapes so let your creativity run wild. You can use different nozzles/tips to create different patterns if you like.

Preheat the oven to 180°C (350°F) Gas 4.

In a large bowl, cream together butter and caster/granulated sugar until light and creamy. Add the cream cheese and whisk in, then add the egg and whisk a little more. Sift in the flour and whisk until you have a very soft dough.

Spoon the dough into the piping/pastry bag fitted with the small round nozzle. On the baking sheet, pipe snowflakes in different patterns. It is important that, although different shapes, the cookies are of a similar size so that they cook evenly. If you want to make some small and some large, use different baking sheets for each size.

Bake for 8–12 minutes until the cookies are firm but take care that they stay pale and do not turn brown. Remove from the oven and leave to cool on the baking sheets.

Dust the cookies with a thick layer of icing/confectioners' sugar to make them white like snowflakes. The cookies should be lifted very carefully, as they will be fragile given the thin lines of each snowflake.

These cookies will keep for up to 3 days in an airtight container.

175 g/1½ sticks butter, softened
60 g/scant ½ cup icing/confectioners' sugar, sifted
180 g/1⅓ cups plain/all-purpose flour, sifted
1 teaspoon pure vanilla extract or ½ teaspoon vanilla bean powder
red sugar sprinkles (optional)
piping/pastry bag fitted with a star nozzle/tip
2 baking sheets, greased and lined

Makes 12

Wreath cookies

Hanging a wreath on a front door is the beginning of Christmas for me – it is a sign to everyone passing my home that the festivities have started inside. These pretty wreath-inspired cookies are made with a buttery Viennese dough sweetened with icing/confectioners' sugar. These are made with vanilla but you can vary the flavour by adding citrus zest or peppermint extract if you prefer. I have hung the cookies with ribbon for a pretty effect but if you want to make them entirely edible, you can tie red liquorice bootlaces into bows instead.

In a mixing bowl, whisk together the butter and icing/confectioners' sugar until light and creamy. Sift in the flour and add the vanilla, then whisk together to make a soft dough.

Spoon the dough into the piping/pastry bag and pipe 12 rings of stars in wreath shapes onto the lined baking sheet. Sprinkle over the red sugar sprinkles, if using. Chill in the freezer for 30 minutes until firm.

Preheat the oven to 180°C (350°F) Gas 4.

Bake the cookies for about 10 minutes until the cookies are just firm. Take care towards the end of cooking as the cookies can turn slightly brown, so you need to remove them before they start to discolour. Leave to cool completely on the baking sheets before looping a ribbon through each one for decoration.

These cookies will store for up to 5 days in an airtight container.

Christmas pudding cookies

FOR THE COOKIES

350 g/2²/₃ cups self-raising/
   self-rising flour
1 teaspoon bicarbonate
   of soda/baking soda
200 g/1 cup caster/
   granulated sugar
grated zest of 1 large
   orange
2 teaspoons ground
   cinnamon
175 g/1¹/₂ sticks butter
3 heaped tablespoons
   golden syrup/light corn
   syrup
100 g/3¹/₂ oz. leftover
   Christmas pudding

FOR THE DECORATION

150 g/5 oz. white chocolate,
   broken into pieces
18 sugar holly decorations
2 baking sheets, greased
   and lined

Makes 18 cookies

**Making Christmas puddings is one of my family's traditions –
every year on 'Stir Up Sunday' we make our puddings to my great
grandmother's recipe – all taking turns to stir and make a wish.
I love the rich flavours of the boozy fruit, oranges and spices. These
cookies, made using crumbled leftover Christmas pudding and
decorated with white chocolate and sugar holly, look truly festive!**

Preheat the oven to 180°C (350°F) Gas 4.

Sift the flour and bicarbonate of soda/baking soda into a mixing bowl. Stir in the
sugar, orange zest and ground cinnamon. In a saucepan, heat the butter and syrup
until the butter has melted. Break the Christmas pudding into small pieces and
stir into the warm syrup mixture. It will soften and dissolve slightly. Stir the syrup
mixture into the flour and whisk in until you have a crumbly dough. Bring the dough
together with your hands.

Divide the dough into 18 pieces and place in small mounds a distance apart
on the baking sheets, as the cookies will spread during cooking. Press the dough
down with your fingertips. Bake in the oven for 10–12 minutes, then remove from
the oven. Leave the cookies to cool on the baking sheets for 5 minutes, as they
will be soft when you remove them from the oven, then using a spatula transfer
them to a cooling rack to cool completely.

Melt the white chocolate in a heatproof bowl resting over a pan of simmering
water, then leave to cool slightly. Spoon the chocolate over the top third of each
cookie in a drizzled pattern so that it resembles a Christmas pudding. Top each
cookie with a sugar holly decoration and leave until the chocolate has set.

The cookies will store for up to 5 days in an airtight container.

Candy cane cookies

200 g/7 oz. natural marzipan
90 g/¾ stick butter, softened
100 g/1 cup ground
    almonds
100 g/scant ½ cup
    self-raising/self-rising flour,
    sifted, plus extra for dusting
1 teaspoon pure vanilla
    extract
red food colouring
2 large baking sheets,
    greased and lined

Makes about 18

**Baked almond marzipan is one of my favourite things and it
makes deliciously festive candy canes in this recipe. The dough takes
food colouring really well which allows you to make beautifully striped
candy canes, just with the dough itself, without the need for icing or
extra decoration. If you want, you could add some sugar holly leaves
to each candy cane, fixing with a little icing.**

Preheat the oven to 150°C (300°F) Gas 2.

Break the marzipan into small pieces and cream together with the butter using an
electric hand-held whisk (or in a stand mixer) until the mixture becomes paste-like.
Add the ground almonds, flour and vanilla and beat to a smooth, soft dough. The
mixture should be soft but not sticky so add a little more flour if needed.

Divide the mixture into two and add a little red food colouring gel to one half, mixing
it in so that it is an even colour.

On a flour-dusted surface, take a small piece of the uncoloured dough and roll it out
into a long sausage shape. Repeat with a same-sized piece of the red dough and roll
out to the same size as the first one. Press the two sausage shapes together to bind the
dough and then twist gently, so that it alternates in a red and white pattern. Use your
fingertips to roll the dough together so that it is smooth, then transfer to one of the
baking sheets and bend into a candy cane shape. Repeat with all the remaining dough.

Bake the cookies for 15–20 minutes until the uncoloured dough just starts to turn
a light golden colour. It is important to cook the cookies on a low heat as in a hot oven
the dough will brown too much and you will lose the red and white coloured effect.
Remove from the oven and leave to cool on the baking sheets.

The cookies will store for up to 5 days in an airtight container.

Treacle house cookies

FOR THE COOKIES

2 heaped tablespoons dark
   treacle/molasses
70 g/²⁄₃ stick butter
200 g/1¹⁄₂ cups plain/
   all-purpose flour, sifted
1 teaspoon bicarbonate of
   soda/baking soda
2 teaspoons ground
   cinnamon
1 egg, beaten
85 g/7 tablespoons caster/
   granulated sugar

FOR THE ICING

450 g/3¹⁄₄ cups icing/
   confectioners' sugar,
   sifted
2 egg whites
1 teaspoon glycerine
1 tablespoon lemon juice
candies and/or edible
   sparkles, to decorate
   (optional)
an assortment of house, tree,
   snowflake and star cutters
2 large baking sheets,
   greased and lined
piping/pastry bag fitted with
   a round nozzle/tip

Makes about 15

These little houses are the perfect Christmas treat – I always have such fun adorning each house differently, using candies and sweets for decoration. My little niece Hunter loves to bake them with me. Use a variety of different shape house cutters to create a whole snow-covered gingerbread village. The number of cookies you make will depend on the size of the cutters you use.

Heat the treacle/molasses and butter in a pan and leave to cool. Place the cooled butter mixture in a mixing bowl with the flour, bicarbonate of soda, cinnamon, egg and sugar, and whisk together. Leave the dough to rest for an hour or so, until it is firm enough to roll out.

Preheat the oven to 180°C (350°F) Gas 4.

On a flour-dusted surface, roll out the dough to about 5 mm/¼ inch thickness. If the dough is still very soft, add a little more flour. Cut out house shapes, trees, stars and snowflakes until all the dough is used up, rerolling as necessary. (Try not to reroll the dough too much though, as it will become crumbly and dry.) Using a spatula, carefully lift the gingerbread shapes onto the baking sheets and bake for 10–12 minutes until firm to touch. Leave to cool slightly on the sheets and when the houses are cool enough to handle you can carefully cut out doors and windows using a sharp knife.

For the icing whisk together the icing/confectioners' sugar, egg whites, glycerine and lemon juice until the icing is light and holds a peak when you lift up the whisk. Add a little more lemon juice if the mixture is too stiff. It is important to whisk the icing for about 3 minutes to beat in as much air as possible.

Spoon the icing into the piping/pastry bag and pipe decorations onto the houses. You can stick gingerbread snowflakes and/or stars onto the roof and pipe lines around the doors and windowframes. Whilst the icing is still soft, add candies or edible white sparkle, if you like. Leave the icing to set before serving or arranging as a decoration.

These cookies will keep for up to 5 days in an airtight container.

Snow scene cookies

60 g/5 tablespoons caster/
  granulated sugar
115 g/1 stick butter,
  softened
170 g/1¼ cups plain/
  all-purpose flour, sifted
  plus extra for dusting
1 tablespoon milk, if needed
blue and green food
  colouring gel
30 g/1 oz. white chocolate,
  broken into pieces
gold sugar star sprinkles
icing/confectioners' sugar,
  for dusting
miniature tree cutter
baking sheet, greased and
  lined

Makes 12

Shortbread dough can be coloured, allowing you to create pretty edible pictures. These little starry night scenes with snow and festive trees make a perfect gift, presented in cellophane bags, tied with ribbon.

Whisk together the sugar and butter until light and creamy. Add the flour and whisk in. If the mixture is too dry add a little milk until the dough comes together in a soft dough. Divide the dough in half. Colour half with a few drops of blue food colouring. Roll the blue dough into a sausage shape, 15 cm/6 inches in length. Take two-thirds of the remaining uncoloured dough and make it into a semi-circle shape the same length as the blue dough. Press the two doughs together and roll on a flour-dusted surface so that the two doughs come together and you have a sausage of dough which is predominantly blue with a white part at the bottom. Wrap the blue and white dough in clingfilm/plastic wrap and roll it into a cylinder shape. Colour the remaining dough green and wrap in clingfilm/plastic wrap. Chill all the dough in the refrigerator for an hour.

Preheat the oven to 180°C (350°F) Gas 4.

Using a sharp knife, slice the cylinder of blue and white dough into 12 rounds and arrange on a baking sheet leaving a small gap between each. On a flour-dusted surface, roll out the green dough very thinly. Using a small tree cutter, cut out small green trees and place on the rounds of cookie dough, positioning them so that the base of the trees are in the white 'snow' and the tops of the trees are in the blue 'sky'. Press down the trees lightly. I suggest two or three trees per cookies for the best effect.

Bake for 10–12 minutes then remove from the oven and leave to cool on a cooling rack.

Melt the white chocolate in a heatproof bowl resting over a pan of simmering water. Leave to cool for a few minutes, then using a cocktail stick/toothpick, put small dots of chocolate in the 'sky' and affix sugar star sprinkles in place. Leave the cookies somewhere cool for the chocolate to set before storing them in an airtight container. Dust with icing/confectioners' sugar before serving.

These cookies will store for up to 5 days in an airtight container.

Garland cookies

160 g/scant 1¼ cup plain/
   all-purpose flour, sifted,
   plus extra for dusting
50 g/½ cup ground almonds
½ teaspoon baking powder
50 g/¼ cup caster/
   granulated sugar
pinch of salt
100 g/7 tablespoons butter,
   softened
1 egg yolk
½ teaspoon ground
   cardamom
1 teaspoon pure vanilla
   extract or ½ teaspoon
   vanilla bean powder
icing/confectioners' sugar,
   to decorate (optional)
an assortment of small
   bauble and/or snowflake
   cutters
2 large baking sheets,
   greased and lined
large round icing nozzle/tip
thin ribbon or string/twine

Makes 40

These pretty little cardamom-spiced cookies are threaded together to make a delicate garland to adorn your Christmas dining table or festive buffet. If you want to give them as a gift, present them in a labelled glass clip-top preserving jar along with a length of pretty ribbon. The cookies can be fragile, so handle them carefully.

In a mixing bowl, whisk together the flour, almonds, baking powder, sugar, salt, butter, egg yolk, ground cardamom and vanilla, until the dough is soft and everything is mixed well. Wrap in clingfilm/plastic wrap and chill in the refrigerator for an hour.

Preheat the oven to 180°C (350°F) Gas 4.

On a flour-dusted surface, roll out the dough to about 5 mm/¼ inch thickness and cut out small bauble shapes or any other festive shapes you like. Place on the baking sheets and bake for 8–10 minutes until crisp.

As soon as you remove the cookies from the oven, use a large round icing nozzle/tip to stamp two holes in each cookie to thread the ribbon through. It is important to do this while the cookies are still warm, otherwise the dough will be too fragile to cut. You can cut the holes before baking, but you will need to make them large as the dough will expand a little on baking which can make the holes too small to thread the ribbon through. Leave to cool.

Once cool, thread the ribbon or string/twine through the cookies, placing them an even distance apart. Dust the cookies with icing/confectioners' sugar, if you like, using a doily to create a pretty pattern. Use the cookie ribbons as decoration.

These cookies will store for up to 5 days in an airtight container.

Stained glass cookies

- 115 g/1 stick butter, softened
- 60 g/5 tablespoons caster/granulated sugar
- 170 g/1¼ cups plain/all-purpose flour, plus extra for dusting
- 10 g/⅓ oz. freeze-dried raspberry powder (or freeze-dried raspberry pieces blitzed to a powder in a food processor)
- grated zest of 1 lemon
- pink food colouring
- a little milk, if needed
- 10 clear fruit boiled sweets/hard candies

large and small decorative star or snowflake cutters

2 baking sheets, lined with silicon mats

small round icing nozzle

ribbon

food processor or blender

Makes 15

Making stained glass cookies is something of a family tradition in my house. One year, I even made a sugar glass dragon cookie for my Dad who is Welsh. They have such a pretty effect against the twinkling lights of a Christmas tree. You can use any boiled sweets/hard candy you like, sherbet lemons have a lovely flavour although the sherbet can cause a few bubbles. My personal favourite is cola cubes, but mainly because that is one of my favourite candies from when I was younger!

For the cookie dough, cream together the butter and sugar and then sift in the flour and add the raspberry powder, lemon zest and a little food colouring and mix until you have a soft pink dough. If the dough is too crumbly, add a little milk. Wrap the dough in clingfilm/plastic wrap and chill in the refrigerator for at least 30 minutes.

Preheat the oven to 180°C (350°F) Gas 4.

On a flour-dusted surface, roll out the dough to about 5 mm/¼ inch thickness and cut out about 15 cookies. Transfer them to the silicon mat-lined baking sheets. When on the baking sheet, cut out shapes from the centre of each cookie. Reroll the dough as necessary and cut out cookies until all the dough is used. Using the small round icing nozzle cut out a hole near the top of each cookie for the ribbon.

Blitz the boiled sweets/hard candies to a fine dust in a food processor and then spoon the sugar dust into the holes on each cookie. Depending on how large the holes are that you make, you may need a few more sweets. Bake for 10–12 minutes, watching carefully towards the end so that the sugar does not start to burn. It will have small bubbles but do not worry as most of these will disappear on cooling.

It is important to leave the cookies to cool on the baking sheet so that the sugar glass sets firm. Once cool, thread ribbon through the holes and hang on your tree or around your house.

These cookies will store for up to 3 days in an airtight container.

gift cookies

FOR THE SNOWMEN

1 egg white

60 g/5 tablespoons caster/
  granulated sugar

FOR THE COOKIES

115 g/1 stick butter,
  softened

130 g/⅔ cup caster/
  granulated sugar

60 g/scant ¼ cup cream
  cheese

60 g/2 oz. Lotus Biscoff
  spread or peanut butter

170 g/1¼ cups self-raising/
  self-rising flour

100 g/3½ oz. white
  chocolate chips

TO DECORATE

140 g/5 oz. white chocolate,
  melted

3 tablespoons icing/
  confectioners' sugar,
  sifted

orange and black food
  colouring gel

piping/pastry bag, fitted with
  a large round nozzle/tip

2 large baking sheets, lined
  with silicon mats or baking
  parchment

cocktail sticks/toothpicks

Makes 14

Meringue snowmen cookies

**These cookies are topped with 3D snowmen made with meringue
resting on a white chocolate snow scene. The cookies are bursting with
white chocolate chips and are flavoured with Lotus Biscoff crunchy
spread which gives a delicious caramel flavour. If you do not have
cookie spread then you can replace with smooth peanut butter instead.**

Preheat the oven to the lowest possible setting, about 130°C (260°F) Gas ½.

Begin by making the snowmen. Whisk the egg white to stiff peaks. Add the sugar, a
spoonful at a time, whisking constantly until the meringue is smooth and glossy. Spoon
the meringue into the piping/pastry bag fitted with the large round nozzle/tip. Pipe 14
circles of meringue about 3 cm/1 inch in diameter on one of the baking sheets. On top
of each of these, pipe a smaller ball for the snowman's body and then a third slightly
smaller one on top for the head. Bake for 45–60 minutes until the meringue is crisp.
Leave to cool on the baking sheet.

Increase the oven temperature to 180°C (350°F) Gas 4.

Whisk together the butter, sugar and cream cheese until light and creamy. Add the
biscuit spread and whisk in. Sift in the flour and whisk in, along with the white chocolate
chips. Place 14 spoonfuls of the dough on the second baking sheet a small distance
apart. Bake for 10–15 minutes until the cookies are lightly golden brown. Leave to cool
for a few minutes on the baking sheet and then transfer to a rack to cool completely.

Spoon a little of the melted white chocolate over each of the cookies and place
a meringue snowman in the centre of each.

In a mixing bowl, mix the icing/confectioners' sugar with a little water and colour with a
few drops of orange food colouring. Use a cocktail stick/toothpick to draw small orange
noses on each of the snowmen. Add a few drops of black food colouring to the orange
icing and then use a second cocktail stick/toothpick to add small black eyes, mouths,
buttons and arms. Leave for the icing and white chocolate to set.

These cookies will keep for up to 3 days, but are best eaten on the day they are made.

Wrapped sweetie cookies

These pretty swirled cookies are inspired by one of my favourite childhood literary heroes, Willy Wonka, the maker of magical candy! Wrapped in waxed paper they look just like your favourite candies. The addition of baking powder will make the cookies spread, so make sure that you place them a good distance apart on your baking sheets, otherwise they will end up stuck together. It is also important to chill the dough well before baking to get the best swirled effect.

125 g/9 tablespoons butter, softened

170 g/generous $3/4$ cup caster/granulated sugar

1 UK large/US extra large egg

1 teaspoon pure vanilla extract or $1/2$ teaspoon vanilla bean powder

225 g/1$3/4$ cups plain/all-purpose flour, sifted

1 teaspoon baking powder

pink food colouring gel

2 baking sheets, greased and lined

24 small pieces of waxed paper

ribbons or string/twine

Makes 24

In a mixing bowl, whisk together the butter and sugar until light and creamy. Beat in the egg and then whisk in the vanilla, flour and baking powder until you have a soft dough.

Divide the dough in half and colour one with a few drops of pink food colouring gel, mixing in well so that the dough is an even colour. If the dough if too soft to handle, add a little more flour.

Wrap the doughs in clingfilm/plastic wrap and chill in the refrigerator for an hour. On a flour-dusted surface, roll out the plain dough into a rectangle (30 x 15 cm/12 x 6 inches) and place on a sheet of baking parchment, lifting carefully using the rolling pin to help you. Next roll out the pink dough to the same size and thickness, and place on top of the plain dough, pressing down gently with your hands. Starting from one of the long sides, roll the dough up in a tight spiral so that you end up with a long sausage shape of dough. Wrap in clingfilm/plastic wrap again and chill in the freezer for a further 30 minutes so that the dough is really firm.

Preheat the oven to 180°C (350°F) Gas 4.

Unwrap the dough and, using a sharp knife, slice the dough into discs about 1 cm/$3/8$ inch in thickness. Place a distance apart on the baking sheets, allowing room for spreading. Bake for 10–12 minutes, then leave to cool on the baking sheets.

When the cookies are completely cold, wrap each cookie in a piece of waxed paper and tie the ends with ribbon or string/twine, so that they look like giant candies. Repeat with all the remaining cookies. These cookies will store for 3 days in an airtight container.

Mini gingerbread houses

125 g/9 tablespoons butter

100 g/½ cup caster/
  granulated sugar

3 heaped tablespoons dark
  treacle/molasses

300 g/2¼ cups plain/
  all-purpose flour, plus
  extra for dusting

1 teaspoon bicarbonate of
  soda/baking soda

2 teaspoons ground ginger

1 teaspoon pure vanilla
  extract or ½ teaspoon
  vanilla bean powder

400 g/scant 3 cups royal
  icing/confectioners' sugar,
  sifted

sprinkles and sugar crystals

2 large baking sheets lined
  with silicon mats or baking
  parchment

9-cm/3½-inch round cutter

templates: 3-cm/1¼-inch
  square; 2.5-cm/1-inch
  square; and an end panel
  with pointed roof that is
  2.5-cm/1-inch square, but
  raising to 4 cm/1½ inches
  at the roof point

piping/pastry bag fitted with
  a small round nozzle/tip

Makes 8

Every Christmas, my little niece Hunter has her birthday at my house – like me she is a Christmas baby! For her birthday the 'birthday fairies' always make her a wintery gingerbread house. You can add candies to decorate the roof, doors and windows, if you like.

Preheat the oven to 180°C (350°F) Gas 4.

Begin by making the gingerbread. In a saucepan, heat the butter, sugar and treacle over a gentle heat until the butter has melted. Sift the flour, bicarbonate of soda/baking soda and ginger into a mixing bowl. Whisk in the butter mixture and vanilla. The dough will be very soft and warm. Transfer to a cool bowl and leave it for about 30 minutes.

The dough should become more firm as it cools. Roll out the dough on a flour-dusted surface to 5 mm/¼ inch thickness and cut out eight circles using the round cutter. Then cut out 16 of each of the templates to make the gingerbread house pieces.

Place the pieces of gingerbread on the baking sheets and bake for 8–10 minutes until the gingerbread is firm. Take care that it does not become too hard, as it will be tough to eat. Leave the gingerbread to cool completely on a cooling rack.

In a mixing bowl, whisk the icing/confectioners' sugar with about 3 tablespoons of water and whisk until you have a smooth, thick icing that holds a peak when you lift the beaters. Spoon the icing into the piping/pastry bag fitted with the round nozzle/tip and pipe tiny windows and doors onto the wall panels of gingerbread.

Because the icing will dry quite quickly it is best to assemble one cookie at a time. Add a little icing to one of the round cookies and press one of the gingerbread panels with the pointed roof into the centre of the cookie. Pipe icing around all the edges of the gingerbread panel and then press the two side panels into the icing so that they attach to the front of the house. Repeat with the back panel. Pipe icing around the top of the house and carefully press the roof panels to complete the house. Pipe a row of icing along the top of the roof where the panels join to seal the roof. Decorate with pretty patterns. Repeat with the remaining houses. These cookies will keep for up to 3 days.

Name place card cookies

115 g/1 stick butter,
 softened
60 g/5 tablespoons caster/
 granulated sugar
170 g/1¼ cups plain/
 all-purpose flour
1 teaspoon pure vanilla
 extract or ½ teaspoon
 vanilla bean powder
a few drops of peppermint
 extract
a little milk, if needed
50 g/2 oz. dark/bittersweet
 chocolate, broken into
 small pieces
crushed candy canes
 or sugar crystal cake
 sprinkles
baking sheet lined with a
 silicon mat or baking
 parchment
8-cm/3¼-inch rectangular
 fluted cookie cutter
piping/pastry bag fitted with
 a small round nozzle/tip

Makes 10

If you are hosting a Christmas Day dinner or a festive supper party, then these peppermint place cards make a unique decoration for your guest table settings. Not only do they look pretty, but they are the perfect accompaniment to coffee at the end of your meal! You can even make a stand for them, by tying three candy canes together, curl-side down.

For the cookie dough, cream together the butter and sugar and then sift in the flour and mix until you have a soft dough. Add the vanilla and peppermint extract. If the dough is too crumbly, then add a little milk. Wrap the dough in clingfilm/plastic wrap and chill in the refrigerator for at least 30 minutes.

Preheat the oven to 180°C (350°F) Gas 4.

Roll out the dough on a flour-dusted surface to a thickness of 5 mm/¼ inch. Using the cookie cutter, stamp out 10 cookies, rerolling the dough as necessary. Transfer to the baking sheet using a spatula and bake for 10–15 minutes until lightly golden brown. Leave to cool on the baking sheet for a few minutes, then transfer to a cooling rack and leave to cool completely.

Place the chocolate in a bowl resting over a pan of simmering water until the chocolate melts. Leave to cool for a short while so that the chocolate cools but is still runny, then spoon into the piping/pastry bag. Pipe a rectangle of chocolate around the edge of the cookie for the border and sprinkle with crushed candy canes or sugar crystals to decorate, tipping away any excess. Pipe the names of your guests in the centre of each cookie with the remaining chocolate. Leave to cool so that the chocolate sets. If you are in a hurry, you can chill in the refrigerator!

The cookies will keep for up to 3 days in an airtight container.

Peppermint bark

115 g/1 stick butter, softened

60 g/5 tablespoons caster/granulated sugar

140 g/generous 1 cup plain/all-purpose flour, sifted, plus extra for dusting

3 tablespoons unsweetened cocoa powder, sifted

1 tablespoon milk, if needed

100 g/3¹/₂ oz. white chocolate, broken into small pieces

1 teaspoon peppermint extract

2 tablespoons crushed sugar candy canes

2 baking sheets, greased and lined

a bark-textured cookie press (optional)

Makes 12

Peppermint bark is one of the most traditional American Christmas candies – sheets of peppermint-flavoured dark and white chocolate topped with candy cane sprinkles. These cookies are inspired by these treats – with a proper bark effect cookie! They are made using a clever 'bark press' which is readily available in cake decorating stores or to order online, but if you don't have a press you can easily create a bark pattern using the tines of a fork, or simply make plain cookies dipped in melted peppermint bark instead. Boxed, they make a beautiful gift.

Preheat the oven to 180°C (350°F) Gas 4.

Whisk together the butter and caster/granulated sugar until light and creamy. Add the flour and cocoa and whisk together to make a soft dough. If the mixture is too crumbly, add a little milk. On a flour-dusted surface, roll out the dough to 5 mm/¼ inch thickness and then cut out fingers of cookie dough about 12 x 3 cm/5 x 1¼ inches in size.

Using a spatula, carefully lift the cookie shapes onto the prepared baking sheets. Press the bark press into the dough to make a bark pattern. If you do not have a bark press, make bark patterns in the dough by scraping it gently with the tines of a fork.

Bake in the preheated oven for 10–12 minutes until the cookies are just firm. Leave to cool on the baking sheets for 5 minutes then move to a cooling rack to cool completely.

Melt the white chocolate in a heatproof bowl resting over a pan of simmering water. Stir in the peppermint extract. Dip the end of each cooled cookie in the melted chocolate and then sprinkle each with the crushed candy canes. Place on a sheet of baking parchment and leave in a cool place to set.

The cookies will store for up to 5 days in an airtight container. It is best to store the cookies flat, in single layers, and between sheets of baking parchment.

Christmas kisses

115 g/1 stick butter,
   softened
60 g/5 tablespoons soft
   dark brown sugar
170 g/1¼ cups plain/
   all-purpose flour, plus
   extra for dusting
24 Hershey's candy cane
   flavoured kisses,
   or similar chocolates
red and white sugar
   sprinkles (optional)
24-hole mini muffin pan,
   well greased
5-cm/2-inch round
   fluted cutter

Makes 24

Hershey's kisses are a popular American candy which come in a wide variety of flavours. They make a perfect filling for small cookie cups, looking pretty with no effort at all. I have used their Candy Cane Flavoured kisses here, as these have pretty red and white stripes. If you do not have Hershey's kisses, you can used other bite-size chocolate candies of your choice to fill the cookie cups. You can use a simple round fluted edge cookie cutter or try a snowflake one, for a more ornate finish.

Cream together the butter and sugar until light and creamy. Sift in the flour and whisk in until you have a soft dough. Wrap in clingfilm/plastic wrap and chill in the refrigerator for 30 minutes.

Preheat the oven to 180°C (350°F) Gas 4.

On a flour-dusted surface, roll out the dough to 5 mm/¼ inch thickness and cut out 24 circles of dough. Press the circles gently into the holes of the mini muffin pan. Reroll the dough and cut out again as needed. Bake in the oven for 10–12 minutes until the cookie dough is golden and crisp. The dough will puff up slightly but will keep an indent in the centre.

Remove the cookies from the pan. They should pop out easily but you can use a teaspoon to slide them out if they are stuck. Place on a cooking rack and, whilst the cookies are still warm, unwrap the Hershey's kisses and place one in the indent of each cookie. Sprinkle with the sugar sprinkles if you wish. Leave to cool.

These cookies will store for 5 days in an airtight container.

Index